I0101572

I Am Human

&

We Are Not Who We Think We Are

Dennis Nappi II

Published by Service of Change, LLC
© 2014 Dennis Nappi II

Edited by: Lori Latimer & Vicky Nappi

All Rights Reserved. No part of this book may be reproduced, scanned, or distributed in any printed or electronic form without permission from the publisher.

ISBN: 978 0 9911375 8 9

www.6SenseMedia.net/IAmHuman

Contents

Introduction

I'd like to start this book by telling you not to be afraid. I'd like to tell you that there is nothing to worry about and everything will be okay. I want to tell you this almost as much as I want to believe it to be true. But I can't.

What I can tell you is that everything has the *potential* to be okay. We have the ability to create a beautiful world, free from the needless suffering and violence that plagues the human condition. We, as humans, have that power. However, in order to access that power we must first face an ugly and terrifying possibility. I'm not saying this to be negative and I'm not saying this to spread fear. This is not my goal. I mention this because in order to move forward, we first must take a step backward.

We need to take a look at ourselves and the world that surrounds us and examine it in every detail. This examination requires an investigation of self and spirit and our connection to everything in existence. It requires hard work, self-criticism, and an honest reflection of ourselves. But most importantly, this examination requires us to identify those things that we fear most. We must identify that which lurks in the shadows of our mind and force ourselves to bring it forward. For it is this fear that keeps us locked in a condition of chaos. It is this fear that manipulates us and divides us against one another. It is this fear that consumes us, and it is this fear that has destroyed us.

In our search for truth, we are often compelled to fight. I first challenge you to *feel* and then evaluate before engaging in battle and you may find that your greatest fight is with yourself. As a society, we tend to identify a problem and turn it into a conflict when a simple change of direction may be all that is needed. We have a right to feel anger and sadness, but those feelings are being used to influence us to cause more harm than good; to turn one problem into many.

An evolution of consciousness and spirit is essential, but I caution you on this path. A simple prayer or sending "love and light" is not going to generate the world you wish to manifest. If not handled properly, your wish for "things to get better" may only serve to reinforce the very problem in which you are trying to change. That being said, I believe this is where our true power lies; it is through our intentions and emotions that we will begin to embody the change we want to see in this world. But it requires work; a dissection of our current system and structure of belief. It requires a willingness to change.

This is the first book of a two-part series. I am offering the eBook version for free because I strongly believe the thought process contained in these pages is of the utmost importance. I am not a guru, spiritual leader, or religious icon. Although I have had spiritual experiences that have given me a hint of what may lie ahead, I am only one voice among countless others. This book is a mere introduction to a lifelong study. If portions of it seem vague or lacking detail, I assure you I dissect them in the second book. My goal here is to hopefully inspire an alternative direction of thought, or to offer reassurance to those already exploring this possibility. I'm not asking you to agree with me. I'm just asking that you keep an open mind.

Contained in this book is my best attempt to explain my feelings and observations accumulated through a series of experiences I've had. I recognize the strangeness of some of the things I describe, but it is because of this strangeness that I feel compelled to share this part of my life. I was trained by the military as an intelligence agent. I ran my own detective agency. I served as a police officer, and now I am a teacher. These accounts are not the fantasies of a lunatic, even though at times I feel insane. I have spent years studying my experiences and those of others, and I have spent just as much time reflecting on the realness of these events. I don't know if my conclusions are valid. I do know, however, that whether I am perfectly sane or not, I am not alone in my conclusions and something needs to change. *Something* is happening. We live in a world where death and suffering are rampant and our current means of prevention, intervention, and prayer have failed. Until we can accept our mistakes, learn from them, and move forward, we will continue to feel the sting of suffering as we walk blindly through the shadow of our existence.

The time for revolution has passed, and we have lost. Our resistance now has new meaning, and it is an internal battle of self. Have the courage to look within and you may be surprised by what you find in the clarity of the world around you...

A Message in the Night

On July 13, 2009, I found myself fighting to fall asleep. My mind raced in a dizzying circle as thoughts blended into a downloaded mess of garbled data. Things I read, experiences I had, and new thoughts I never had before swam in a chaotic soup of mind. My chest burned as if an open wound was absorbing everything around me. The thoughts that raced through my head, however, were different. They were *feelings* that originated in that burning storm within my chest and resonated throughout my body. My mind then worked to turn those feelings into thoughts and words I could understand. The problem was, there was too much information in my head and it was flowing too fast for me to process. My intuition was on overload, forcing me into a specific direction of pensive understanding. I felt as if I understood, but when I tried to think about what I was feeling, nothing made any sense. Finally around 2:00 a.m., I gave into the struggle. Sleep was avoiding me and I knew if I didn't make sense of the chaos in my mind that I may never sleep again.

It's all connected. We are not what we think we are. They are out there. Food. Prisoners. Religion. Spirituality. It all serves a purpose, but we have failed to recognize what that is.

My mind continued to spin as I jumped out of bed and hurried down the hall to my home office. I grabbed a pen and began scribbling my thoughts as they came to me, and to my surprise, instead of a garbled mess of random information, the confusion poured through my pen in a logical, coherent format. Five-and-a-half pages later, I had a document that not only expressed so much of what I was *feeling*, but presented me with an understanding of something I had questioned my entire life. It started me on a journey of insight into who we are, and what we have become.

There is a connection between *everything* in existence; a force that flows through all things. Life is bountiful and beautiful, but requires the very essence of life to survive. In order to sustain life, the consumption of life is needed. This was made quite clear to me as I transcribed this essay, and my reflection of it was terrifying.

Through my explanation, I came to understand that humans were no different than other lifeforms. We depend on life in order to sustain our own existence. We raise livestock and grow crops only to slaughter and consume them. With this understanding, my concept of good and evil changed. To a chicken, we must seem like horrible, devilish ghouls, but to the family dog we must seem like loving, caring members of the pack. This was not what terrified me, however. My fear grew from the realization of the possibility that although we may believe we are the lords of this world, our existence may serve a much darker agenda to a force hidden from our awareness, *as food for something else...*

Them

I am still amazed at the doubt that exists in my mind. To this day, I question the validity of my experiences and first-hand accounts, even with the knowledge that other people whom I have never met share similar experiences and have drawn similar conclusions. *Something* is out there and it is using us to satisfy its cravings.

Since early childhood, I've had memories of waking in the night in a state of paralysis. My mind would be awake and alert, and at realizing my frozen condition, panic would set in. The more I squirmed, the tighter and more restricted my muscles would become. As my struggle ensued, I'd realize that I was not alone. Off to my side there would stand a figure hiding in the shadows, just at the edge of my periphery. It was a heavy presence that seemed to cause the air around me to press harder on my body. Fear would consume me, and I'd fight harder to break free, causing the tightness in my body to become so severe my breathing would grow labored. I'd force air in and out of my nose, trying to keep oxygen flowing to my lungs. Terrified, I'd sense this creature move toward me, when suddenly exhaustion would set in. I'd stop worrying about this presence and instantly drift peacefully to sleep as if nothing was there at all.

In my early twenties, I developed a habit of writing down everything I could remember about an experience immediately after it occurred. As so many other experiencers report, despite the power of these encounters, memory of them sometimes fades into the fog of nothingness. So I've kept my journals, and I am grateful for them. While reviewing my entries, I have noticed a recurring trend: Fear. It is a fear unlike anything I have ever experienced that seems to be induced within me by Them. It's as if they want me afraid in order to harvest something from me. In one of my entries, I wrote that I thought "they were taking something from me, either energy or spirit."

I kept this possibility to myself for the thought of my energy being harvested sounded insane. For the longest time, even people reporting abductions didn't seem to give any indication of energy harvesting. But I had too many conscious experiences where I felt energy being taken from my chest as a product of the fear that I was feeling. It turns out, I was not alone in my sentiments after all.

In his final book, *The Active Side of Infinity*, author Carlos Castaneda tells of his discussion with Mexican shaman Don Juan Matus about a predator that feeds on the energy of man:

They took over because we are food for them, and they squeeze us mercilessly because we are their sustenance. Just as we rear chickens in chicken coops, gallineros, *the predators rear us in human coops,* humaneros. *Therefore, their food is always available to them.*[1]

I came across Castenada's book years after I drew my own conclusion about energy harvesting, shortly after the death of my father. Having drawn this conclusion prior to reading his book, I felt nauseous with fear at the possibility that my suspicions may in fact be true. More importantly, Castenada's words almost identically mirrored the essay I wrote that sleepless night in July of 2009, right down to the chicken-coop metaphor. This "coincidence" corroborated and therefore lent credibility to my own intuition that I was experiencing a real event. Whatever afflicts us while we sleep is draining us of our very essence. Just as Morpheus demonstrated to Neo that he was nothing but a battery, we too

1-Castenada, Carlos, The Active Side of Infinity (New York: HarperCollins, 1998), 219.

are being used as a source of energetic nourishment...

Nothing is What it Seems

As far back as I can remember, I have felt driven by a deep, hidden force. I remember being just five-years old explaining to my mother that I was on a "mission," even though I wasn't quite sure what that mission was. It felt important, it felt powerful, and *I* felt chosen. I don't mean chosen as in the Holy Messiah sense. Simply, I've always felt there was something I was predestined to do and if I didn't figure out what it was, my life would be meaningless. This feeling guided and pulled me in thought and choice as I tried to gain understanding as to what I was supposed to do, and who or what expected me to do it.

I was raised Catholic, and as I went through the sacraments, I tried to find guidance through God and my faith. But the strength of my internal beacon weakened whenever I would walk down my fixed-religious path. I felt muffled and misguided, despite the strong faith my family and I had.

Religion failed to explain my nightly encounters, and prayer failed to bring clarity to my turmoil and fear. Books, however, brought me comfort. As I'd get lost in the pages of someone's experiences with Them, I felt a sense of hope. I felt a possibility of understanding and I felt peace, which was something religion had failed to bring me. It was the search that drove me, and it was this search that resonated strongest with my life's mission. So I resigned myself to trust in my intuition and follow it anywhere it led me, despite having no clue what I was looking for.

In 1999, I was 19 years old. I was attending college to study Criminal Justice and had been recently trained as an Intelligence Analyst by the US Army for my National Guard unit. One particular Friday night, my friends and I were searching for something to do. We debated for a while until finally deciding to catch a late show at our local movie theater. *The Matrix* was playing, and I had no idea what it was about. I sat mesmerized and completely dumbfounded throughout the entire film. It made no sense to me at all, yet part of me understood exactly what the movie was trying to convey. Adrenaline calmly flowed through my body in measured pulses as Neo began to discover the truth. I shook with possibility and hope that somewhere in this film lay an answer to the question I did not know; an explanation of the mission I was born to complete. As Neo met Morpheus, time slowed and almost froze for me. *He's talking to me,* I thought. His words rang out of the complicated plot with a harmony of clarity I could not ignore:

Let me tell you why you're here. You're here because you know something. What you know you can't explain, but you feel it. You've felt it your entire life. That there is something wrong with the world, but you don't know what it is; but it's there, like a splinter in your mind, driving you mad. It's this feeling that has brought you to me.[1]

I understood that feeling Morpheus was describing. He was explaining the feeling I had that I was on a mission, which meant that someone else felt that same drive. It also meant I was not alone in my search. It was such an intense feeling of needing to know, that at seeing this movie I felt a renewed interest in understanding what it meant. I was so taken by the film, yet so perplexed by what it was trying to present. Machines, agents, altered reality - none if it made any sense, but I knew there was something important in its content.

In an attempt to find meaning, I actually ran an Internet search to find *my* Morpheus - a similar teacher who was going to summon me in the night to offer a pill of knowledge; to tell

11

1- Dir. Andy Wachowski & Larry Wachowski. The Matrix, DVD (Warner Bros. Pictures, 1999)

me what it was that I have always wanted to know. He would guide me through a series of life-changing processes that would ultimately result in my expulsion from this garden of illusion after I ate from the fruit of knowledge he offered me.

My Morpheus, however, wasn't out there. I received no late-night contacts and no magic pills. I was simply left alone with my thoughts and my books, trying to learn all I could, guided by that internal beacon that sometimes pulled from unknown places deep inside me.

The Search

The Matrix validated my feelings and my search. It showed me that even though it was presented as fiction, there was someone else out there who had the same feelings and pull as me. Whether that meant we were crazy, or actually being driven by a deeper force, was yet to be seen. But I needed to know either way. I still wasn't even quite sure what I was searching for, but I knew there was a feeling within me that seemed to offer guidance. It was a slow teacher, leading me to one piece of information at a time. Being anxious and eager, I wanted everything at once, but what I came to realize was that each thing I learned took time to process and understand. My belief system, my personal values, and my understanding of the way the world worked were gradually being dismantled and rebuilt. The information was jarring, sometimes quite upsetting, and at times sent me deep into a depression of hopelessness. It's not easy learning that so much of your life has been built around a lie; that the things you trust as good are actually working against you. It's easy to get sucked into the pessimistic hold of that realization and hate everything around you for what it really is: A system designed to keep you down. "A prison for your mind," as stated in *The Matrix*.

As I mentioned previously, I was raised Catholic. I grew up knowing I was a sinner and not worthy of heaven. I knew that if I committed a mortal sin, or a series of sins throughout my life, without confessing them to my priest and my God, then my soul would be condemned to an eternity of suffering in Hell. I also knew that the suffering experienced on this planet was God's will. When I questioned this concept, I was told that it was something I was not meant to understand and that it was all a part of Gods plan. God loved me, and in the end it would all be worth it because I was earning an eternity in paradise. I swallowed this logic even though it confused me, for to question it was itself a sin. During this time of my life, fear was the motivational force behind my spirituality and relationship to God.

In 1998, my best friend was killed by a drunk driver, and everything changed. Scott was the most caring, giving, understanding, and intelligent person I have ever known. He embodied goodness and lived his life the way a good Christian should, except for one tiny thing: Scott was an atheist. He told me he just couldn't accept a belief in God because his mind was too scientific for that concept. Upon hearing of his death, I worried for my friend. I worried that since he did not accept a Christian faith that he would be denied access to Heaven and possibly sent to Hell. This thought then expanded, and I began to wonder about all the people in the world, especially the indigenous populations, that still existed in remote areas without Christ. One question turned into several, and before I realized it, my faith began to rapidly crumble.

Were the native people of the world all condemned to an eternity of suffering, even though they never had an opportunity to learn of Christianity? Was that why so many of them were slaughtered during the Christian expansions and inquisitions throughout history? Would a loving God, responsible for creating *all* people, want them to kill each other? Furthermore, would that same loving God condemn some of his people to an eternity of suffering? If God is such a loving God, then why do we have war? Why are innocent children killed? Why is there so much anguish? Does free will really require God to stand back and allow the innocents to suffer so needlessly? If God is so powerful, then why does he allow Satan to reap havoc among us?

As my faith quickly deteriorated, my desire to connect with a spiritual path strengthened. I still wasn't sure where this internal drive was leading me, but I knew one thing: If someone as genuinely good as Scott would be denied a place in Heaven, then Heaven was no place I wanted to be.

Having denounced my Catholic faith and freed myself from the mental burden of sin and the fear of a loving God, my heart felt free and open. My soul felt free from its bondage and I experienced a sense of spiritual freedom I had never known.   But where was it leading me?

Nature

Having gained a little more clarity in my search, I set my sights on better grasping the concept of God in hopes of finding a spiritual path to direct my life. Believing that God was a supreme deity, responsible for the creation of all life, I felt compelled to look at *all* life to see if I could further comprehend my own path and the human condition. During this journey, I had come to an understanding that all life was sacred, and all life warranted respect. I developed an opposition to killing things, and took great pride in capturing and releasing the occasional spider that would find its way into the dark corners of my home. This ideology felt wonderful. I experienced a closer connection to Nature and to all life around me, until one day I found a small wasps' nest on my property.

My initial instinct was to kill the wasps with toxic chemicals, and protect myself and my two dogs from their painful stings. But killing would counteract my new-found philosophy of respecting all living things. In examining this situation, I tried to understand why I wanted to kill these creatures. The answer was quite clear: they were dangerous. They built a nest on my property and if provoked, even by accident, they would react violently against me, causing terrible pain throughout my body with their stinging rage. It seemed like a valid argument, but then I wondered: *What if I was living in the garden of something more powerful? Would it be fair for this Keeper of the Garden to terminate my existence simply because of my peoples' tendency toward violence and destruction?*

The mere thought of this powerful being trying to kill me ignites a violent defensive instinct in me. I am the wasp, and I am the Keeper of the Garden.

I was so bothered by this concept that I spent several days trying to find the right course of action for these wasps. In the process, I began to understand more of what was written in my essay that chaotic night in 2009. I read articles and watched videos, and what I learned was that Nature could be extremely cruel. Wasps, like every other creature, required life to sustain life. Some species of wasp even invaded other colonies of insects to kill them and steal their hoards. This wasn't the beautiful, loving balance of Nature I had come to embrace. It was a cruel, violent world that *required* death in order to sustain life, and I was no different. *As above, so below. I am the wasp and I am the Keeper of the Garden.*

In the end, I made the choice to kill the wasps because of their *potential* for violence. I felt terrible for doing it, but I was too afraid to risk an experiment of cohabitation, considering the painful consequences of misjudgment. Through this process of understanding, I wondered:

Why did God design our existence to require the death, and sometimes suffering, of all forms of life in order to survive? If God was so loving, why was the very basis of life dependent on death and why did religion seem to reinforce the importance of such suffering?

I Am The Wasp...

Reflection

For the longest time, I felt pulled to answer an essential question. Although it was a question I could not formulate into words, I knew I needed to find its answer. I understand that question now, and go into great detail explaining it in the second book. This question is so simple yet massively compelling in design. To fathom it is to unlock the secrets of our existence and may quite possibly reshape our entire way of life. I don't know the origin of the source that has guided me; whether it be a part of my own spirit, something separate from myself, or a combination of the two. But it is there, as real as you and me.

I have witnessed many things in this lifetime; things that are impossible to ignore or forget. Through my time as both a soldier and police officer, I've known hardship. I've heard the cries of citizens as they reminisced about their country's civil war. There was death and destruction, dismemberment and trauma. They lost mothers and fathers, brothers, sisters, and children. As a police officer I've been in homes of the recently deceased; a mess of suicide and pain with no explanation why. I've seen abused children, battered women, and the ugliness of addiction and mental illness. Lastly, as a son, I've witnessed the death of my own father. I heard his labored breath and cries of pain. I watched him fight for life as we begged him to let go, and during that process, I felt something. It was something I had always known was there, but never fully accepted. As my father suffered his cancerous death, I had a feeling burn deep within my chest. It was a feeling I had grown to recognize, through many terrifying nights alone. It was a feeling, as I came to understand, that meant *They were there...*

The Essay

This is the essay that resulted from the chaotic mess of feeling and thought on July 13, 2009. It's in its original format, and the only corrections I have made have been for spelling errors and paragraph separation. As time goes on, I understand its message more and more. It is titled, I Am Human because it is a reflection of the human condition. I hope you find insight from it, and I hope together we can find meaning. This essay is the basis for my next book, I Am Human: Food for the Archons, where I explore not just my own experiences in detail, but the experiences of others with Them. I am trying to understand just what they are, what they want, and what we can do about them. There is more to our existence than we realize. As a part of that existence, there are some terrifying possibilities. But with an honest search for knowledge and understanding, I believe we can make a difference. I hope you'll join me.

I Am Human

I am tired but I cannot sleep, yet I am sleeping but not awake. I am hungry and I want to eat. I am human.

I have been lying in bed for about two hours. I'm exhausted but I cannot sleep. My mind has been racing for quite some time, but I'm not sure how long. Was it just today? Just this evening? Or has it been much longer? I feel like I've been questioning and pondering since I was first able to think. But tonight feels different. Is it because I am so tired, almost delirious? I've been here before. I feel as if I am on the edge of something. It feels huge, yet insignificant at the same time. I feel as if the world as I know it is about to change forever. Is it my perception that is changing, or is it the world? Which would be worse? Everything I see is fitting into the larger picture in way's I've never viewed before, yet we move blindly on.

I was thinking about my fish tank. I have four Tiger Barbs. They swim all day long, sleep almost upside down, and enjoy eating the flake food I provide them. It seems as if they recognize me because they come out of hiding when I'm getting ready to feed them. Before I throw the food in they begin racing around the tank with excitement. What is their understanding of reality? What is their perception? I will never know. Do they understand the concept of war? Of global warming? Of terrorism and crime? Do they understand death or happiness? I do not know, but I would think that they do not understand them as we humans perceive them, yet all can still affect them. Their world consists of swimming in a tank and being fed. What happens if I stop feeding them? Do they understand that I am not feeding them – or do they simply wonder why they can't find food floating on the top of the water? If these four fish were to die, would it affect any of us? Sure, I would be saddened by their passing, but would a man living in a town thousands of miles away be affected as well? Would he even know that my four fish had died? Their purpose is merely one of entertainment. Yes, I love them. I created a world for them. I feed them and care for them. But what significance do they truly hold?

What about the many animals, for example chickens, we raise in captivity only to destroy and consume them once they have reached maturity? They grow to depend on us, to raise them, feed them, and to keep them safe. Do they understand their purpose is simply to indulge our cravings? To be a flavorful delicacy? And what of the bird who is raised to maturity, slaughtered, and then dropped on the floor from the dinner table in its deliciously dead and moist rich state? We humans would most likely discard this carcass of bird meat in the garbage without a second thought. So what purpose did this bird serve? To live, be slaughtered, and then thrown in the garbage.

And if these birds became aware of their plight – If they learned of the fate in which they had no choice – would they mount a resistance? Would one bird or many birds be able to defend themselves against the onslaught of their hungry caregivers and providers? Or would they come to embrace their destiny and find a sort of spiritual enlightenment in knowing they were the food for their caregivers, the Gods of their understanding?

This topic is driving me crazy. I have moments of clarity, were I think I understand all of it, the entire big picture; and then it is gone. All of it, and I feel as if I have to start all over again. From the first thought to the last – trying to understand what it was I had learned for only a moment before it was wiped from my memory once again. You see, I fear it is too great a concept. Too much to bare for my preconditioned mind. Too much to understand for my growing soul. So I accept what I have seen and believe in what I am told. But I question. Something is wrong. Something is not right. Men have questioned before me and my hope is that many will long after me. But something is awry. Something doesn't fit. We may never know the answers to the questions we have. We may find false truths and no truths, and we may never know at all...

"Free your mind."
"What is real?"
"Do you think that is air you are breathing?"

These are questions and advice provided by a man to a young savior in the popular *Matrix* movie. Although disguised by the façade and glamor of Hollywood lights and stardom, the movie inspired me. Without my realizing it, it sparked to life something that has been growing inside my mind and soul for quite some time. Was this the goal of the writers? I may never know. But writers wish to inspire; to leave a mark in the minds of the readers and participants of their work. And inspire me they did. I had to watch the movie over a dozen times to even begin to understand what it was saying. In the end, the message is quite clear. It is simply: Reality is not real. Does that make it wrong? Does that make it evil? It alludes to the fact that we are prisoners and victims of our own reality, a reality that is being generated by a greater force, a higher power. A force that pulls the shades over our eyes to hide the truth about our existence – about who we are and our purpose in life. It hides the pain and cruelty of reality, which may be too much for the human soul to carry. In the movie our minds are fed life as our bodies lay lifeless in suspended animation, leaving us unaware, unnoticed, and unimportant. We are kept alive for one simple purpose: Food. Without the energy our bodies produce, the machines who keep us could never survive. But if one of us was to fall off the tree of life, would it matter? Or would they still continue to have their seemingly endless supply of human-powered nutrition? As for those who became aware of our plight, a resistance was mounted against the machines. But did it make a difference?

The movie followed, metaphorically, many religious texts ranging from the story of Christ to the Mayan Popol Vouh story of creation. In the end, peace was achieved between man and machine. But we were not freed. In order for all of humanity to survive, the majority needed to stay connected to the machines, trapped in the electronically programmed reality. And for the machines to survive, they continued to hold captive their crops of humans, generating the power food they so badly needed for nourishment. What really changed? A character in the first movie who mirrored the betrayer Judas stated: "Ignorance is bliss." Was he right?

I recently found a video online to a song I enjoy called Hayling. The graphic video shows many clips capturing the struggle of life, the triumph of survival, and the tragedy of death while the lyrics cycle: "Don't think about all those things we fear, just be glad to be here." It captures animals engaged in a mortal combat for life.

One needs simply to escape to sustain life, whereas the other needs to hold on long enough to consume the victim in its clutches. It's graphic, slow, and disturbing to watch an animal die. To see the life drain slowly out of a small furry body. It saddens me, and I feel pains deep within my spiritual heart in watching these battles. Even on video, the struggle is immense and almost unbearable. Since watching it, this video has haunted me. It has opened my mind to a reality I knew but never understood. It has shown it to me in a different light, and I'm not sure I like what I have found. Life is about death. Life is violent and life is cruel. As humans we try to evolve and adapt. We try to be kind and at peace with our surroundings. We protect our environment and the many species who share this planet. But at the end of the day, we eat. To eat, we kill, or at least support the action. Some of us gave up meat, and eat only the plant life on this planet. Our reality tells us this is better, but a question still rings in the air. Because they do not scream, does that mean they don't feel pain? Or sorrow? Something has to die or suffer in order for us to live. To live in balance is to care for the creatures that in turn nourish our bodies. We show respect and pay homage by cultivating our crops and our livestock. But we kill them to live. Life requires death, and the cycle continues on. This does not make it wrong and it does not make it right. It simply is.

So what is our reality? Is it what we understand? Is there more? I continue to search for an answer – an answer that many men before me have sought, and many men after will seek. Realizing the violence in survival, no matter how far removed from it we are, has been a challenge, at the very least. But what scares me even more – what scares me more than realizing how cruel this web of life can truly be at times, and how blind we truly may be – is the thought that splinters in the back of my brain. If so many animals depend on us to survive: If so many creatures are oblivious to their purpose in our lives, like the fish in the tank or the chickens on the farm, then what is our greater purpose? History tells us we are the top of the food chain. But history was written by men. Our leaders preach to us about a God; a God who is loving and caring, forgiving, and just. But these are the words of men. My fear is, not that there is no God up above. My fear is that what if we hold a greater purpose that is outside our capacity for understanding or perception of reality? What if we swim aimlessly in this fish tank we call Earth? What if we walk blindly through our coup of a planet that has us conveniently penned into an engineered reality we have come to accept? At times I feel as if I know the truth, yet have no way of possibly explaining it. These thoughts, however, are not what truly scares me. It's the thoughts I haven't yet had that I can't possibly comprehend. Those are the ones that absolutely and completely terrify me...

References

Castenada, Carlos, The Active Side of Infinity (New York: HarperCollins, 1998), 219.

Dir. Andy Wachowski & Larry Wachowski. The Matrix, DVD (Warner Bros. Pictures, 1999).

About the Author

Dennis Nappi II is an American author living in Pennsylvania. Early in his career, Dennis served as an intelligence soldier for the army and worked as a police officer. Dennis holds a master's degree in education and has been a special-education teacher for over a decade.

Dennis has dedicated his focus to better understanding the potential of human intuitive abilities. He has shared his experiences, interviews, and research surrounding psychic phenomena and the paranormal in his books, podcast, videos, and website. He is currently exploring his own abilities through remote viewing, reiki, and meditation. In his spare time, Dennis can often be found on an adventure in nature with his 3 young children.

You can learn more about Dennis and his work through his website, **6SenseMedia.net** and on his podcast, *The Seiker Podcast,* where he spends considerable time exploring topics that include Psychic Phenomena, Remote Viewing, UFO Disclosure/ET Contact, and the AI Integration with the Human Mind and Society.

Never Stop Questioning, Keep an Open Mind,
& Let Your Intuition Be Your Guide!

Book 2 Now Available!

I Am Human, Food for the Archons
Humanities Psychic Connection, Simulated Realities, Parallel Worlds, and the Manipulation of Mankind

Please visit:

www.6SenseMedia.net/Archons

Book 2
Our greatest vulnerability is the source of our forgotten power...

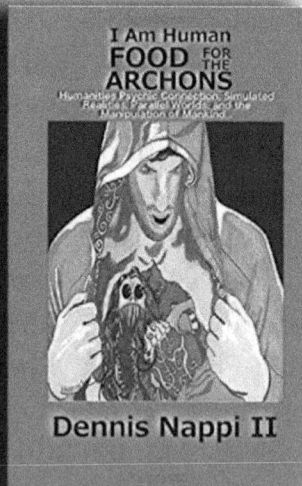